故園畫憶

庚寅中秋
韓磐澄題

《故园画忆系列》编委会

名誉主任: 韩启德

主　　任: 邵　鸿

委　　员: (按姓氏笔画为序)

万　捷	王秋桂	方李莉	叶培贵
刘魁立	况　晗	严绍璗	吴为山
范贻光	范　芳	孟　白	邵　鸿
岳庆平	郑培凯	唐晓峰	曹兵武

故园画忆系列
Memory of the Old
Home in Sketches

丝路遗迹

Relics Along the Silk Road

刘洪　李钦曾　绘画　撰文
Sketches & Notes by Liu Hong　Li Qinzeng

学苑出版社
Academy Press

图书在版编目（CIP）数据

丝路遗迹 / 刘洪，李钦曾绘画、撰文. — 北京：学苑出版社，2017.9
（故园画忆系列）
ISBN 978-7-5077-5327-1

Ⅰ.①丝… Ⅱ.①刘…②李… Ⅲ.①钢笔画—作品集—中国—现代②新疆—概况 Ⅳ.①J224.8②K924.5

中国版本图书馆CIP数据核字（2017）第226918号

出 版 人：	孟　白
责任编辑：	洪文雄　周　鼎
编　　辑：	陈柯宇
出版发行：	学苑出版社
社　　址：	北京市丰台区南方庄2号院1号楼
邮政编码：	100079
网　　址：	www.book001.com
电子信箱：	xueyuanpress@163.com
联系电话：	010-67601101（营销部）、67603091（总编室）
经　　销：	全国新华书店
印 刷 厂：	北京赛文印刷有限公司
开本尺寸：	889×1194　1/24
印　　张：	5.5
字　　数：	120千字
图　　幅：	93幅
版　　次：	2017年9月北京第1版
印　　次：	2017年9月北京第1次印刷
定　　价：	45.00元

目 录

自 序　　　　　　　　　　　　李钦曾

吐鲁番地区

交河故城·全景	3
交河故城·民居遗址	4
交河故城·官署遗址	5
交河故城·墓葬	6
雅儿湖石窟群	7
苏公塔·院外	8
苏公塔·院内	9
高昌古城·土墙	10
高昌古城·外城	11
高昌古城·内城	12
高昌古城·宫城遗存	13
高昌古城·宫殿遗址	14
回鹘晚期佛塔遗址	15
台藏塔遗址	16
胜金口佛寺	17
吐峪沟石窟	18
连木沁吐尔尕列子	19
二塘沟烽火台	20
阿拉沟烽燧	21
柏孜克里克石窟	22

哈密地区

小南湖佛塔遗址	25
白杨沟佛寺遗址	26
哈密回王陵·回王坟	27
哈密回王陵·小拱拜	28
盖斯墓	29
塔尔阿特麻扎	30
巴里坤古城·远景	31
巴里坤古城·德胜门	32
巴里坤古城·城墙	33
三塘湖烽燧遗址群	34

阿克苏地区

苏巴什佛寺·西寺	37
苏巴什佛寺·东寺	38
苏巴什佛寺·远景	39
苏巴什佛寺·城墙	40
库木吐拉石窟	41

默拉纳额什丁麻扎	42	阿克斯皮尔古城残墙	70
库车大寺	43	乌宗塔提遗址	71
森木赛姆石窟	44	流水墓地	72
克孜尔石窟	45	喀拉墩故城	73
钟鼓楼	46	圆沙古城	74
		艾提卡尔大清真寺	75
喀什地区		大清真寺	76
徕宁城	49	牛头山佛寺遗址	77
高台民居	50	尼雅遗址·古城	78
艾提尕尔清真寺·正门	51	尼雅遗址·墓葬	79
艾提尕尔清真寺·塔楼	52	尼雅遗址·佛殿	80
香妃墓·正面	53	尼雅遗址·官署	81
香妃墓·背面	54	安得悦古城	82
阿巴哈加麻扎	55		
三仙洞石窟遗址	56	**昌吉回族自治州**	
莫尔佛塔寺院遗址	57	土墩子烽火台	85
阿勒通鲁克麻扎·全景	58	土墩子清真寺	86
阿勒通鲁克麻扎·必修克	59	北庭西大寺	87
加曼清真寺	60		
棋盘石窟	61	**巴音郭楞蒙古自治州**	
加曼清真寺	62	铁门关遗址	91
脱库孜萨来佛寺遗址	63	拉依苏汉代烽燧遗址	92
石头城	64	拉依苏唐代烽燧遗址	93
吉日尕尔汉唐驿站遗址	65	营盘古城遗址	94
		小河墓地·女性墓	95
和田地区		楼兰古城·三间房遗址	96
热瓦克佛塔	69	楼兰古城·佛塔遗址	97

孔雀河古墓沟	98	**伊犁哈萨克自治州**	
米兰佛寺	99	陕西回族大寺	107
奎克衙门（和静县民族博物馆）	100	六星街	108
察吾乎古墓群石围石室墓	101	伊犁将军府	109
奥巴尔墓地石人	102	吐虎鲁克麻扎	110
黄庙	103	惠远古城	111
		昭苏县草原石人	112

Contents

Forward   Li Qinzeng

Turpan Area

Ancient Jiaohe-Panorama	3
Ancient Jiaohe · Residential Site	4
Ancient Jiaohe · Government Office Site	5
Ancient Jiaohe · Tombs	6
Yaer Lake Grottoes	7
Sugong Tower · Exterior	8
Su Gong Tower · Interior	9
Iduqut Shahri · Locality	10
Iduqut Shahri · Outer Town	11
Iduqut Shahri · Inner Town	12
Iduqut Shahri · Palace Remains	13
Iduqut Shahri · Palace Site	14
Uighur—Late Pagoda Site	15
Taizang Tower Site	16
Shengjinkou Buddhist Temple	17
Tuyugou Grottoes	18
Lianmuqintuergaliezi	19
Ertanggou Beacon Tower	20
Allah Gou Beacon Tower	21
Bezkilik Grottoes	22

Hami Prefecture

Small South Lake Pagoda Site	25
Baiyanggou Buddhist Temple Site	26
Kumul Khanate Mausoleum.Kumul Khanate Grave	27
Kumul Khanate Mausoleum · Small Gongbai	28
Geithner's Tomb	29
Thalat Mazar	30
Ancient Balikun · Distant View	31
Ancient Balikun · Deshengmen Gate	32
Ancient Balikun · Town Wall	33
Santanghu Beacon Tower Sites	34

Akesu Prefecture

Subashi Temple · West Temple	37
Subashi Temple · East Temple	38
Subashi Temple · Panorama	39
Subashi Temple · Town Wall	40
Kumtura Tula Grottoes	41

Molana Ershending Mazar	42		Jirigaer Han-Tang Inn Site	65
Kuqa Temple	43			
Senmusaimu Grottoes	44		**Hotan Prefecture**	
Kizil Grottoes	45		Rewake Pagoda	69
Bell and Drum Tower	46		The Ancient Town Wall of Akespier	70
			Wuzongtati Site	71
Kashgar Prefecture			Liushui Cemetery	72
Laining Town	49		Karadong Site	73
Gaotai Residents	50		Ancient Yuansha Town	74
Aitigaer Mosque · Main Entrance	51		Aitikar Grand Mosque	75
Atigaer Mosque · Tower Building	52		Grand Mosque	76
Xiangfei Tomb · Front	53		Niutou Mountain Buddhist Temple Site	77
Xiangfei Tomb · Rear Side	54		Niya Site · Jingjue Ancient Town	78
Abahajia Mazar	55		Niya Site · Tombs	79
Sanxiandong Grottoes	56		Niya Site · Buddhist Hall	80
Moer Pagoda Temple Ruins	57		Niya Site · Government Office	81
Aletongluke Mazar · Panorama	58		Ancient Andeyue Town	82
Aletongluke Mazar "Bixiuke"	59			
Garman Mosque	60		**Changji Hui Autonomous Prefecture**	
Chessboard Grottoes	61		Tudunzi Beacon Tower	85
Garman Mosque	62		Tudunzi Mosque	86
Tuokuzisalai Buddhist Temple Site	63		North Court West Temple	87
Stone Town	64			

Bayingol Mongolian Autonomous Prefecture

Iron Gate Site	91
Han Dynasty Layisu Beacon Tower Site	92
Tang Dynasty Layisu Beacon Tower Site	93
Ancient Yingpan Town Site	94
Xiaohe Cemetery · Female Tomb	95
Loulan Ancient Town · Three Rooms site	96
Ancient Loulan Town · Pagoda Site	97
Peacock River Ancient Grave Ditch	98
Milan Buddhist Temple	99
Quike Government Office	100
Chawuhu Ancient Stone Tombs	101
Obaer Cemetery Stone Man	102
Huang Temple	103

Ili Kazak Autonomous Prefecture

Shaanxi Hui Grand Temple	107
Six Star Street	108
General Ili's Mansion	109
Tuhuluke Mazar	110
Ancient Huiyuan Town	111
Grassland Stone Men in Zhaosu County	112

自 序

本书以丝绸之路新疆段历史遗迹的美术呈现为主要表现内容。时至唐代,"西域"的地理范围已包含今天新疆维吾尔自治区的大部分地区。清乾隆时期,"西域"始被称作"新疆";至嘉庆时,"西域"这一名称已经完全被"新疆"一词取代。荣新江教授认为丝绸之路是"以中国为根本的古代东西交往的各条通道"。丝绸之路进入西域后,大致分成中道、南道、北道三条路线,来自东方的丝绸、瓷器、纸张、茶叶、樟脑、明矾、漆器和来自西方的棉花、香料、皮货、雕像、琥珀、青金石等物资贸易,以及文化、语言的交流与传播;民族的迁徙与融合也大致沿着这三条道路来进行。

两汉以来在西域这片广袤的土地上,先后兴起的小国家、城邦多达五六十个。鄯善、吐鲁番、北庭、伊犁、龟兹、于阗、尼雅、楼兰、喀什、图木舒克等地存在的城邦或国家的文明在新疆乃至中华民族的历史上都产生过重大而深远的影响。塞种、月氏、匈奴、乌孙、羌、藏、突厥、回鹘、蒙古、粟特、吐火罗、维吾尔、哈萨克等民族都在西域遗留下了众多的遗迹。萨满教、祆教、佛教、摩尼教、景教、伊斯兰教也曾深深地影响着西域人民的精神信仰和日常生活,留下了诸多的宗教遗迹。在新疆广袤的大地上,还保留着大量的古城、石窟、寺庙、麻扎等多种形态的历史文化遗迹,这都是本书在遴选表现对象时需要重点考虑和兼顾的。

截至2016年,新疆共有113处全国重点保护单位,其中古遗址49处、古墓葬28处、古建筑14处,石窟寺及石刻9处,近现代重要史迹及代表性建筑13处。本书精心遴选101处最能代表新疆文化特色和文化成就的历史遗迹,其中和田地区14处、巴音郭楞蒙古自治州13

处、喀什地区16处、吐鲁番地区25处、阿克苏地区9处、昌吉回族自治州3处、哈密地区11处、伊犁哈萨克自治州6处、克孜勒苏柯尔克孜自治州4处。

笔者亲自到遗迹、遗物现场考察写生，感受西域文化的浑厚、多元与开放。本书采用钢笔速写画的形式来表现，希望读者能直观地了解和领略丝绸之路新疆段的古代风貌。晋陆机曾言，"丹青之兴，比《雅》《颂》之述作，美大业之馨香。宣物莫大于言，存形莫善于画。"本书的价值即在于此。最后，深深感谢学苑出版社洪文雄编辑为本书的出版所提供的建议与帮助。

李钦曾

Forward

This book is mostly based on an artistic representation of historical relics along the Xinjiang section of the Silk Road. During the Tang Dynasty (618-907), the "Western Region" of China encompassed most of the current Xinjiang Uygur Autonomous Region. During the Qing Dynasty (1644-1911) Jiaqing Period (1796-1821), the name "Western Region" was replaced by the word "Xinjiang". The term "Silk Road" refers to "The ancient routes between the East and the West centered around China". The Silk Road was roughly divided into middle, south and north routes in the Western Region.

Since the West and East Han Dynasties period (202 B.C.- 220 A.D.), this vast Western Region has seen the rise of over 50 small countries. Their civilization has had a significant, far-reaching influence upon Xinjiang and even the history of China; its numerous historical and religious relics left in Xinjiang are the focus of this book.

Xinjiang has a total of 113 national key protection units, of which there are 49 ancient sites, 28 ancient tombs, 14 ancient buildings, 9 grottoes and stone inscriptions as well as 13 other historical sites and representative buildings of early modern times. For this book, we carefully selected 101 of the most representative historical sites featuring Xinjiang cultural characteristics and achievements.

I personally went to the ruins of the sites to sketch and feel the depth of the area's culture which is presented as Chinese drawing with neutral pen, intended to help readers intuitively understand the ancient civilization of the Xinjiang section of the Silk Road. I deeply appreciate the assistance of Hong Wenxiong of The Academy Press with the book.

Li Qinzeng

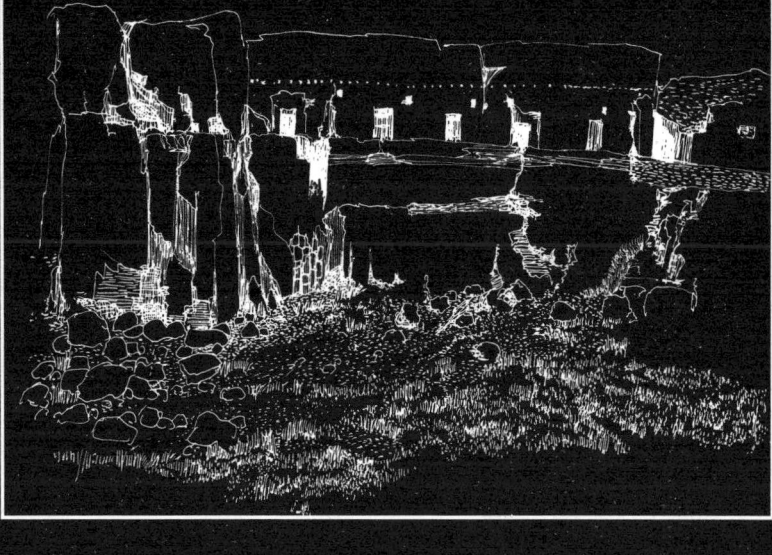

吐鲁番地区
Turpan Area

交河故城·全景

　　位于吐鲁番市亚尔乡，距离吐鲁番市区13千米，在一座平面呈柳叶形的岛形台地上。始建于公元前2世纪，因河水分流绕于城下，故称"交河"。曾是车师前国的都城，在南北朝和唐朝时达到鼎盛，9～14世纪由于战火逐渐衰落。元末察合台时期，因吐鲁番一带的战火，交河城银毁损严重被废弃。图为交河故城遗址全景。

Ancient Jiaohe-Panorama
Located on a willow leaf-shaped earthen platform in the AI township, it is 13 kilometers from the city of Turpan. Due to river diversion around the city, it is called "Jiaohe", i.e. "crossing river". The sketch is a panorama of the river.

交河故城·民居遗址

　　交河故城的建筑布局主要由三个部分组成：贯穿南北的中心大道把居住区分为东、西两部分，大道北端是一座寺院，以它为中心构成了北部的寺院区。大道东区南部为大型民居区，北部为小型居民区，中部为官署区；大道西区除大部分为民居外，还分布有手工作坊。图为交河故城民居遗址。

Ancient Jiaohe · Residential Site

Jiaohe is composed of three main parts: the east and west residential areas that are divided by a central road from north to south and the northern temple area at the northern end of the road. The south of the eastern area is a large residential area, the north is a small residential area, and the central part is a government office area. Most residential areas and handicraft workshops are located in the western area. The sketch shows the ruins of ancient Jiaohe.

交河故城·官署遗址

　　交河故城的建筑全部由夯土筑成，形制布局则与唐代长安城相仿。城内市井、官署、佛寺、佛塔、街巷，以及作坊、民居、演兵场、藏兵壕、寺院佛龛中的泥菩萨都有发掘。图为交河故城官署遗址。

Ancient Jiaohe · Government Office Site

The buildings, all made of rammed earth, include markets, government offices, temples, workshops, dwellings, and 101 pagodas. The temple in the northern part of town covers an area of 5,000 square meters and has a drain well. The sketch shows a government office site.

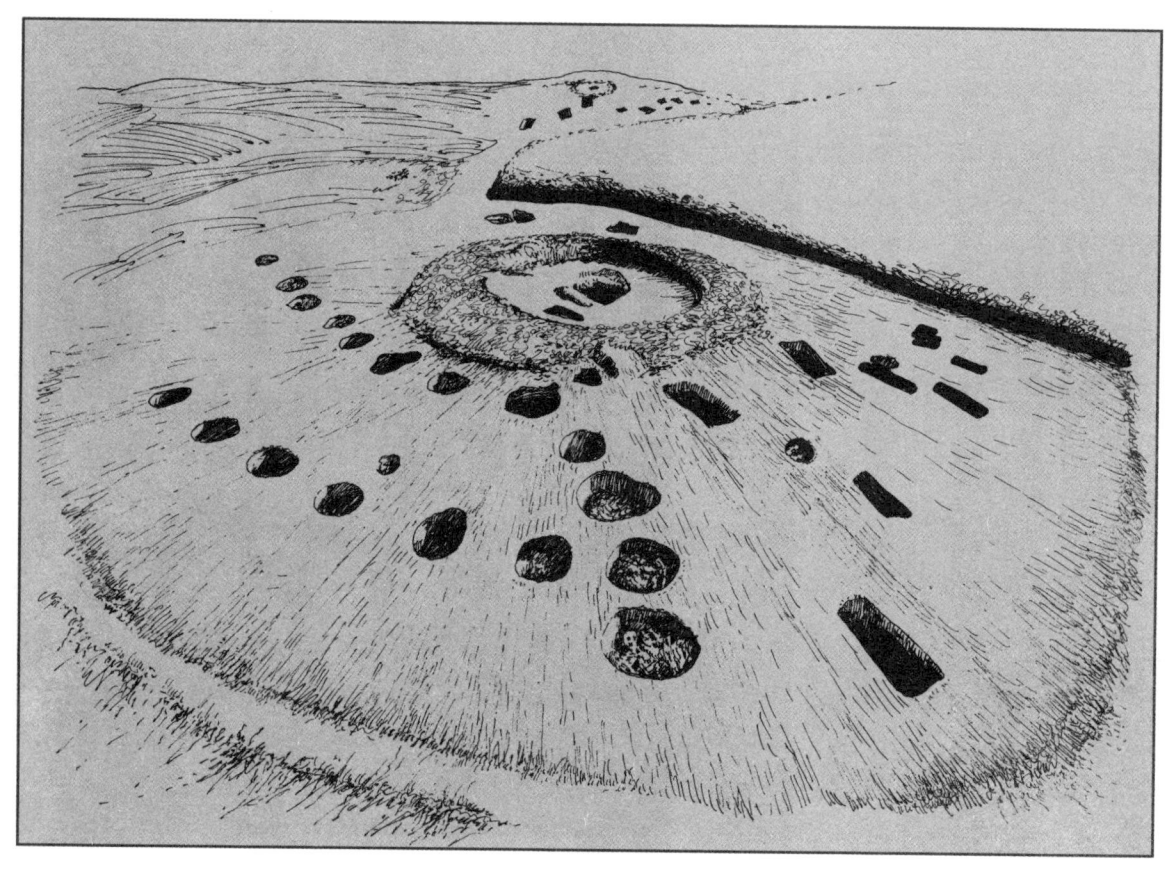

交河故城·墓葬

　　位于交河故城雅尔乃孜沟北的台地上，为汉代前后车师国贵族的墓葬。墓葬地表有圆形石堆，墓室为长方形土坑竖穴，死者多为仰身直肢，陪葬品有床、木棺等器物。图为交河故城沟北一号墓地16号墓葬。

Ancient Jiaohe · Tombs
The tombs are located on a platform of the north of Yaernaizigou village in Jiaohe. The burial chambers are rectangular and vertical, thus the dead are mostly standing leaning with straight limbs. Funerary objects include beds, wooden coffins and other objects. The sketch shows the 16th tomb of cemetery No. 1 of ancient Jiaohe.

> 雅儿湖石窟群

　　古称"西谷寺",位于交河故城雅尔乃孜沟西,始建于5世纪车师前国时期,9世纪以后回鹘人又重新绘制其壁画。目前遗存七座洞窟,为纵券顶长方形形制。

Yaer Lake Grottoes

In ancient times called "West Valley Temple", it is located west of Yaernaizigou village of Ancient Jiaohe. Built during the Cheshiqian state circa (500A.D.), seven caves remain.

苏公塔·院外

又称"额敏塔",位于吐鲁番市东郊2000米处的葡萄乡木纳尔村,建成于清乾隆四十三年(1778年),是额敏和卓及其儿子苏赉满为报答清王朝的知遇之恩和表达对真主的虔诚而修建的一座塔。塔下建有清真寺,该清真寺是新疆伊斯兰古建筑中现存规模最大的一座建筑。图为苏公塔外景。

Sugong Tower · Exterior
Also called "Emin Tower", built in 1778, it is located in Munal Village of Grape township, two kilometers from the eastern outskirts of Turpan City. Under the tower stands a mosque, the largest existing ancient Islamic style building in Xinjiang. The sketch shows the exterior of the tower.

| 苏公塔·院内 |

　　苏公塔塔身呈圆柱形，由青灰色条砖砌筑而成，高44米，塔基直径为10米，塔身下大上小，呈圆锥形。塔内有螺旋形台阶72级通往顶部。塔身周围不同方向和高度，设有14个窗口。塔的表面分层砌出三角纹、四瓣花纹、水波纹、菱格纹等15种几何图案，具有浓厚的伊斯兰建筑风格。图为苏公塔内景。

Su Gong Tower · Interior

The cylindrical 44-meter high tower is constructed of steel-gray rectangular bricks. It has a 10-meter diameter foundation with a conical body large at the lower part and smaller at the upper part. The tower has a 72-step spiral staircase to the top and 14 windows in varying positions and heights. The sketch shows the tower's interior.

高昌古城·土墙

位于吐鲁番市东南约40千米处的哈拉和卓乡附近,始建于公元前1世纪,由西汉王朝在车师前国境内的屯田部队所建。曾因"地势高敞,人庶昌盛"而得名。现存高昌壁、高昌郡城、高昌国都、高昌回鹘国以及中央地方州郡等历史遗迹。

Iduqut Shahri · Locality
Located in Khara-khoja township roughly 40 kilometers from southeast Turpan, it was built in the first century B.C., by Tuntian troops within the territory of Cheqian state during West Han Dynasty (206 B.C.-24).

高昌古城·外城

高昌古城外城周长约5000米，城墙墙基厚12米，高11.5米，由夯土筑成，间杂少量土坯。南面有三个城门，东、西、北面各有两个城门。西、北两面城门保存情况最好，目前可见瓮城。除"可汗堡"等政治性建筑遗迹外，绝大部分为佛塔、佛寺、僧房等佛教建筑。

Iduqut Shahri · Outer Town

The outer town is about five kilometers in circumference and its wall, with a 12-meter thick footing and 11.5 meters high, is made of rammed earth. There are three gates in the south wall and two gates each in the east, west and north. Those in the west and north are best-preserved. Other than "Khan Fort" and other political architectural relics, the vast majority of structures are pagodas, Buddhist temples, monk dormitories and other Buddhist buildings. The sketch shows the outer town.

高昌古城·内城

  高昌古城的内城在外城中间,城墙全为夯土,西、南两面保存较好,其建筑年代较外城为早。内城北部正中有一平面不规则略呈正方形的小堡垒,当地称"可汗堡"。堡内北面的高台上有一高达15米的夯筑方形塔状建筑物;西边有一座双层建筑物,现仅存地下部分。

Iduqut Shahri · Inner Town

The inner town is in the middle of outer town. Its walls are all of rammed earth. The west and south walls are better-preserved and built earlier than outer town. There is a small fort with irregular square plane in the middle of the north part of inner town. The sketch shows the inner town.

高昌古城·宫城遗存

  高昌古城平面呈不规则的正方形，由外城、内城和宫城三部分组成，总面积约200公顷。宫城在最北面，留存许多高大的殿基，一般高3.5~4米左右，外城的北墙是宫城的北墙，内城的北墙是宫城的南墙。图为宫城部分建筑遗存。

Iduqut Shahri · Palace Remains
Iduqut Shahri plane is an irregular square, formed by outer and inner towns and the palace. The palace lies in the town's northernmost part. The north wall of outer town is that of the palace, and the north wall of the inner town is the south wall of the palace. The sketch shows the palace remains.

高昌古城·宫殿遗址

位于高昌古城北部"可汗堡"的北面，现有高达15米夯筑而成的方形塔状建筑物一座、地上地下双层建筑物一座。在此曾发掘出一通"北凉承平三年沮渠安周造寺功德碑"（445年）。图为宫殿遗址。

Iduqut Shahri · Palace Site

In the north of "Khan Fort" north of Iduqut Shahri, stands a square tower-like piled building, 15 meters high, with one storey above and one below ground. The sketch shows the site.

| 回鹘晚期佛塔遗址 |

　　位于高昌古城的东南角,由土坯垒砌而成,残高七米左右,始建于11世纪,台基呈方形,塔身呈圆形,现残存三层佛龛。该佛塔为高昌回鹘晚期的文化遗存。

Uighur—Late Pagoda Site

Located in southeast corner of Iduqut Shahri in Turpan, the round adobe pagoda, originally built in the 11th Century, is 7 meters high with a square base. Three-layer shrines remain.

台藏塔遗址

位于吐鲁番市三堡乡，距离高昌古城1000米，始建于6世纪的麹氏高昌时期。遗址平面呈长方形，面积达1200平方米，由土坯夯筑而成，中间夹杂圆木，残高20米，呈四棱台状，自下而上逐步收缩。现东、北两面清晰可见佛龛，龛内残留塑像痕迹。

Taizang Tower Site

Built in the 6th Century in Sanbao township of Turpan City, one thousand meters from Iduqut Shahri, the site plane is rectangular, with an area of 1,200 square meters, and constructed of adobe, mixed with logs in the middle. It is 20 meters high, sizing down from the bottom to the top.

胜金口佛寺

位于吐鲁番市胜金乡的木头沟口谷地,距离高昌古城5000米左右,始建于晋代。主要遗存和遗物有晋代至元代的寺庙、佛塔、藏经室、佛头像以及早期突厥语文、回鹘文书写的佛经故事、摩尼教文献等。

Shengjinkou Buddhist Temple

Located in Murtuq Valley of Shengjin Township, Turpan City, it was originally built during the Jin Dynasty (265-420), about five kilometers from Iduqut Shahri. Major relics include temple, pagoda, scripture chambers, Buddha-head statues dating from the Jin Dynasty to the Yuan Dynasty (1265-1368).

吐峪沟石窟

位于鄯善县吐峪沟乡，距离高昌古城十千米左右。开凿于5世纪前后，是吐鲁番地区开凿最早的石窟群。吐峪沟石窟由东区、西区及霍加麻扎组成，沿沟谷两侧南北约500米范围之内分布，其中主要窟群有四处。存世洞窟总计94个，保存了3～9世纪的佛教壁画。

Tuyugou Grottoes

Located in Tuyugou Township, Shanshan County, they were excavated around the 5th century AD, about 10 kilometers from Iduqut Shahri. These are the first grottoes to be excavated in the Turpan area. They consist of east, and west areas and the Hogan Mazar, where Buddhist frescoes from the 3rd to the 9th Centuries are well preserved in the 4 main caves.

连木沁吐尔尕列子

又名"连木沁大墩",位于鄯善县连木沁乡吐尔尕列子村,始建于唐代。边长17.8米,为正方形的烽火台。"吐尔尕列子"是维吾尔语,"土尔"意为"烽火台"或"瞭望塔","尕列子"意为"坎儿井"。

Lianmuqintuergaliezi

Also known as "Lianmuqin Dadun", located in Tuergaliezi Village, Lian Muqin Township, Shanshan County, it was a square beacon tower originally built during the Tang Dynasty (618-907). It is 17.8 meters wide.

> 二塘沟烽火台

　　位于鄯善县连木沁乡，始建于唐代。为土坯建筑，平面呈方形，剖面呈梯形，现仅存东底，占地面积约765平方米。中央为空室，中部有券顶洞室，塔体外壁有洞孔。

Ertanggou Beacon Tower

Located in Lianmuqin Township of Shanshan County, this adobe building was built during the Tang Dynasty (618-907). Foundation is square, and its section is trapezoidal. Now only the east wall foundation, covering an area of about 765 square meters, remains. The central part is empty, with Quanding caves in the center and holes in the outer wall.

阿拉沟烽燧

　　位于托克逊县城西56千米，始建于唐代。烽火台是以砾石为主、土坯为辅的城堡式建筑，东西长约30米，南北长约31米，加上城外围墙，总面积1000余平方米。烽火台呈梯状，高十米。该遗址是东疆唯一的一座由石头垒筑的烽燧遗址。

Allah Gou Beacon Tower

Located 56 kilometers west of Toksun county, it was originally built during the Tang Dynasty (618-907). In the west and south is a cliff 16 meters high. Beacon towers are castle-style buildings made of gravel and adobe. The tower is in the northwest corner of the castle and is its tallest building. This is the only beacon site in eastern Xinjiang piled with stones.

柏孜克里克石窟

　　位于吐鲁番市东北约40千米的火焰山峡谷内木头沟河西岸，始建于5世纪，大部分洞窟为麴氏高昌和唐西州时期所建。"柏孜克里克"在维吾尔语中有"山腰"之意。窟群散布在河谷西岸约1000米范围内的断崖上，分三层。现存洞窟83个，其中有壁画的40多幅，保存壁画总面积1200平方米。

Bezkilik Grottoes

Located on the west bank of Mutougou River in Flaming Mountain Canyon, about 40 kilometers northeast Turpan City, it was originally built in the 5th Century A.D. Grottoes are arrayed on the cliffs in a range of one kilometer from the west bank of valley. It has three layers of grottoes. There are more than 40 murals in the 83 caves totaling an area of 1,200 square meters.

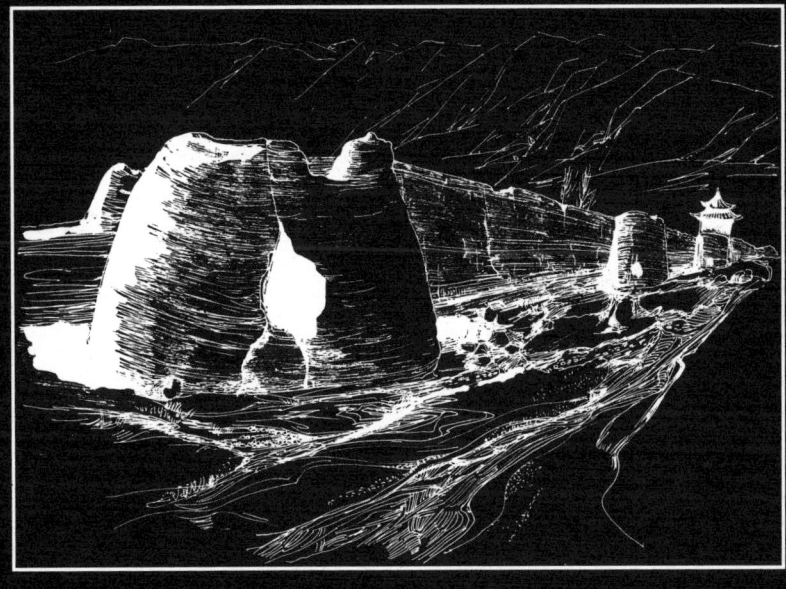

哈密地区
Hami Prefecture

小南湖佛塔遗址

位于哈密市花园乡小南湖村，始建于唐代。佛塔保存完整，由塔基和塔身组成，残高12米。塔基为夯土筑就，平面呈正方形；塔身为土坯垒砌，共分三层，上小下大，纵剖面为梯形，每层皆用土坯砌出塔檐。底层门面向西南。塔内平面呈方形，为穹窿顶，内壁绘有壁画。

Small South Lake Pagoda Site

Located in Small South Lake Village, Garden Township, Hami City, it was built during the Tang Dynasty (618-907). The pagoda is 12 meters high with a large lower part and a small upper part. Its longitudinal section is trapezoidal. Its square plane footing is of rammed earth. The Pagoda is made up of adobe totaling three layers.

白杨沟佛寺遗址

位于哈密市柳树泉农场白杨沟村东1000米处的白杨河上游，始建于唐代。白杨河水自中部流过，将其分成东西两部分，当地维吾尔族人称为"台藏"。寺院主要遗存在白杨河西岸，主体建筑残高15米，墙厚一米，分前后两室，以甬道相连，主室居后，顶为穹隆形，内残存一坐佛，高8.2米。

Baiyanggou Buddhist Temple Site

Built during the Tang Dynasty (618-907) in the upper reaches of Baiyang River, one thousand meters east of Baiyanggou Village, Liushuquan farm, Hami City, the monastery is the major remnant on the west bank of the river. The main building is 15 meters high with one-meter-thick walls. It has two rooms in front and back, connected by a corridor. Its domed main room behind houses has a seated Buddha.

哈密回王陵·回王坟

又名"哈密王墓",位于哈密市西郊回城沙枣井,始建于清康熙四十八年(1709年)。陵墓建筑群占地面积约1.3公顷,共分三部分,原有五座木结构亭式小拱拜和艾提卡大清真寺。埋葬着七世回王伯锡尔等40人。图为回王坟。

Kumul Khanate Mausoleum.Kumul Khanate Grave
Originally built in 1709 in Shazaojin Village, Huicheng Township, the western outskirt of Hami City, the tomb complex covers an area of about 1.3 hectares. It is divided into Kumul Khanate Grave where 40 people are buried including Kumul Khanate VII Wang Bucier, five small wooden pavilion-style tombs such as Gongbai ancient Kumul Khanate tomb, and Aitika Grand Mosque. The sketch shows Kumul Khanate Grave.

哈密回王陵·小拱拜

　　现存的两座小拱拜，东部一座为九世回王沙木胡索特拱拜；西部一座为台吉拱拜。九世回王拱拜融汇了满、蒙、汉、伊斯兰建筑风格，整个建筑分为三层，上为蒙满式盔顶建筑，中为汉式八角攒尖顶，底部垣墙及四周用亭柱支撑。图为哈密回王陵的小拱拜。

Kumul Khanate Mausoleum · Small Gongbai
The existing small Gongbai is divided into three layers, of mixed Manchu, Mongol, Han and Islamic architectural styles. The top part is the Manchu and Mongol style helmet-roofed building. The middle is a Han-style octagonal roof with a spire; its walls supported by pillars. The sketch shows the small Gongbai of Kumul Khanate Mausoleum.

盖斯墓

又名"绿拱拜"或"圣人墓",位于哈密市大营门村,1939年建于哈密星星峡,1945年移到现址。墓主人盖斯是唐代一位来华传教的伊斯兰教教士。建筑为伊斯兰式建筑,高约十米,下部方形,上部为拱式圆顶,顶部用绿色琉璃瓦镶砌,四周有廊檐。

Geithner's Tomb

Also named "Green Gongbai" or "Sage Grave", it is in Hami's Dayingmen Village. Built in 1939 in Hamixingxingxia Town and moved to this site in 1945, it is an Islamic building, about 10 meters high; the lower part is square, the upper part is an arch dome, and the top has green glazed tile inlay all surrounded by corridors.

塔尔阿特麻扎

位于伊吾县千山哈萨克自治乡,距离县城130千米。始建于清朝末年,伊斯兰教传教士塔尔阿特葬于此。该麻扎为庭院式建筑,依山而建,包括大门、木栅栏围墙、主墓室以及为牧民礼拜而修建的房屋等。

Thalat Mazar

Located in the Kazakh Autonomous Township, Yiwu County, 130 kilometers from the county, it was originally built in the late Qing Dynasty (1644-1911). It is a courtyard-style building, built near the hillside, consisting of gates, wooden fence walls, a main tomb and houses built for the herdsmen to attend religious services.

巴里坤古城·远景

  又名"满汉城",为相邻的两座土城,位于巴里坤哈萨克自治县巴里坤镇的西部。汉城始建于清雍正九年(1731年),当年城中心筑钟鼓楼,并放射出四条大街,南大街筑兵营,东西北三条大街均为民房,城内有演兵校场、火药局。满城筑于清乾隆三十七年(1772年),为驻扎于此的满营官兵及家眷所建。当时城内有四条大街,共有官署、库房、兵丁及家眷住房3000多间。

Ancient Balikun · Distant View

Also called "Manhan Town", it is located west of Balikun Town, Balikun Kazakh Autonomous County. The ethnic Han city was built in 1731; the ethnic Man city was built in 1772. The sketch presents a distant view of Balikun.

巴里坤古城·德胜门

古城有四座门楼，城墙上有城垛3600个，城外有炮台七座、马面八座，城周围挖有护城河，城外设吊桥四座。现存西城门及瓮城，德胜门是在清代城墙遗址的基础上新修建而成的，城内原有建筑已不存在。图为巴里坤古城德胜门。

Ancient Balikun · Deshengmen Gate

The town has four gatehouses, each wall of which has 3,600 battlements. The town outside has seven forts, eight "horse faces", and is traditionally called "City Desk". There is a west town gate and an urn city. Deshengmen Gate was built on Qing Dynasty (1644-1911) wall ruins. The sketch shows Deshengmen Gate.

巴里坤古城·城墙

　　汉城平面为长方形，面积有1.2平方千米，墙高6.8米，顶厚四米，底厚六米，除西城墙保存完好外，其余三面城墙均有程度不同的破坏和残缺。满城于辛亥革命后，只剩下四面城墙，目前这里修建有工厂、机关、部队营房和住房，现在东、南、北三面城墙还完好。图为巴里坤古城城墙。

Ancient Balikun · Town Wall
A Han town plan is rectangular area of 1.2 square kilometers. Its walls are 6.8 meters high. The well-preserved west wall is four meters thick at the top and six meters at the bottom. Man town's walls are intact. The sketch shows the wall of ancient Balikun.

三塘湖烽燧遗址群

位于巴里坤哈萨克自治县,由多座烽燧组成,最早的烽燧修建于唐代,现存的绝大部分都是清代修建的。基座呈正方形,燧体为向上收缩的菱形柱,均为夯土建筑,夯土中夹杂有红柳枝,并多用圆木构架。

Santanghu Beacon Tower Sites

The many towers are in Balikun Kazakh Autonomous County. The earliest beacon was built during the Tang Dynasty (618-907). Most of the existing towers were built during the Qing Dynasty (1644-1911).

阿克苏地区
Akesu Prefecture

苏巴什佛寺·远景

苏巴什佛寺的城墙用土坯垒砌而成，厚约三米，残高约10.8米，周长约318米，是晋唐时期的历史文化遗存。佛殿的建筑平面呈方形，大佛殿内尚有小佛堂，壁上见有佛龛。大殿西侧为僧房和禅房，大殿北约50米处的临河断崖丘状山体的石壁上，保存有当年开凿的十余座洞窟。图为苏巴什佛寺远景。

Subashi Temple · Panorama
The architectural plane of the Buddha Hall is square; the adobe walls are about 3 meters thick, 10.8 meters high and 318 meters in circumference. These are historical and cultural relics of the Jin and Tang dynasties (265-420 and 618-907). The sketch is a panorama view of Subashi Temple.

苏巴什佛寺·西寺

苏巴什佛寺又名"昭怙厘大寺""苏巴什古城",位于库车河两岸的山麓台地上,距离库车县城约23千米。始建于汉代,该遗址分东西二寺,地跨库车河两岸,总面积约18万平方米。"苏巴什"是维吾尔语,意为"水头"或"龙口",是新疆现存规模最大的地面塔寺遗址。图为苏巴什佛寺的西寺。

Subashi Temple · West Temple

Built during the Han Dynasty (202 B.C.-220 A.D.), on the piedmont platform on both sides of Kuqa River, about 23 kilometers from Kuqa County, it is divided into the east and west temple, with an area of 180,000 square meters. The sketch shows Subashi West Temple.

{ 苏巴什佛寺·东寺 }

　　苏巴什佛寺的东寺依山而筑，南北长约500米，东西宽约140米，主要由北、中、南三座佛塔组成。南塔保存较好，塔身圆形，土坯筑成，塔顶呈穹形，塔身中部有一圈柱洞，塔周有围墙，墙上有10余个佛龛。最北一座耸立在半山腰，可俯视全寺遗址；大部分遗迹都集中于地势起伏不平的河岸上。图为苏巴什佛寺的东寺。

Subashi Temple · East Temple

Subashi East Temple built near a hillside, is about 500 meters south to north and about 140 meters east to west. It is composed of three pagodas on the north, middle and south. The south tower is well preserved. The north one stands on the hillside, from which the entire temple site can be seen. Most of the remains are concentrated on the undulating riverbank. The sketch shows Subashi's East Temple.

苏巴什佛寺·城墙

　　苏巴什佛寺的西寺南北长700米，东西宽190米左右。主要由北、中、南三塔；佛殿和南部寺院组成。北塔周围分布有佛洞，内残存壁画和龟兹文题记。佛殿位于遗址中部。南部寺院遗址略呈方形。大寺四周有围墙。东墙和东南墙都已塌毁，西墙及北墙保存较好。图为苏巴什佛寺的城墙。

Subashi Temple · Town Wall

Subashi's west temple is 700 meters long north to south and about 190 meters east to west. It is composed of three towers (north, middle and south), Buddha Hall and the southern temple. The sketch shows the temple wall.

库木吐拉石窟

位于渭干河谷东岸的确勒塔格山麓的断崖壁上,距离库车县城约30千米,开凿于4~11世纪。石窟分南北两区,已编号洞窟有112个,南北蜿蜒750米。现存壁画数千平方米,以描绘大乘佛教内容为主,壁画艺术"唐风"较浓。亦有少量雕塑,还有大量的龟兹文、汉文、回鹘文的题记。

Kumtura Tula Grottoes
Originally constructed during the 4th century AD and completed around the 11th century in the cliffs of the Queletage foothills on the east bank of the Weigan Valley, about 30 kilometers from Kuqa County, the grottoes are divided into north and south sections, with 112 numbered caves winding for 750 meters north to south. The Mahayana Buddhist murals cover an area of thousands of square meters.

默拉纳额什丁麻扎

　　又名"默拉纳和卓墓",位于库车县新老城之间,建于明代。"默拉纳"在维吾尔语中是"圣人后裔"的意思。麻扎建有祠宇、分祠门、祠堂、墓门和墓室四部门,全部以绿色琉璃砖装饰。祠西廊下有匾额,上书"天方列圣"四个大字。两旁有题记,为清光绪七年(1880年)李蕃所题。

Molana Ershending Mazar

Built during the Ming Dynasty (1368-1644) between the old and new city, Kuqa County, its name, "Mulana", in the Uygur language means "sage descendants". In Mazar, aspects of interest include temple, sub-temple door, ancestral hall, tomb gate and burial chamber, all decorated with green glazed tiles.

库车大寺

　　位于库车县城黑墩巴扎的最高处，距库车新城4000米，始建于15世纪，初始为土结构的寺院，17世纪改作木结构寺院，1923年重修后遇大火焚毁，现存寺院为1931年建成。寺院面积1165平方米，是新疆境内第二大寺。主体建筑有两部分，一是大寺主体，内有旋转楼梯至寺顶，全为砖木结构；二是供信徒礼拜时使用的大殿。

Kuqa Temple

Originally built in the 15th century AD at the highest place in Hedun Bazaar Town in Kuqa County, four kilometers from the Kuqa new town, the temple covers an area of 1,165 square meters, the second largest temple in Xinjiang. The main building includes the monastery, a spiral staircase to the top of temple, and a hall for people to worship. All structures are of brick and wood.

森木赛姆石窟

　　位于库车县东牙哈乡克里西村西北的确勒塔格山麓，开凿于5世纪。"森木赛姆"维吾尔语意为"细细的泉水"。洞窟沿自西北向东南流向的小溪的两岸开凿，可分为东、西、南、北、中五个区，已编号洞窟有52个。森木赛姆石窟的主要文物是玻璃杯、菱格因缘故事画、佛涅盘像和举哀天人图。

Senmusaimu Grottoes

The grottoes were constructed during the 5th century AD in Queletage hill northwest of Kelixi Village, Dongyaha Township, Kuqa County. "Senmusaimu" in Uyghur language means "thin spring". The 52 grottoes along the site, excavated on both sides of a stream from northwest to southeast, can be divided into east, west, south, north, and middle areas.

克孜尔石窟

又名"克孜尔千佛洞或赫色尔石窟",位于拜城县东南的克孜尔镇,开凿于3世纪。现存已编号洞窟269个,壁画约一万平方米。洞窟形制有中心柱窟、大像窟、方形窟和僧房窟;壁画题材有本生、因缘、佛传故事、天相图、伎乐飞天、供养人等。图中雕塑为鸠摩罗什铜像。

Kizil Grottoes

Also called "Kizil Thousand-Buddha Caves or Hesheer Grottoes", they were excavated in the 3rd century AD in Kizil Town southeast of Beaching county. There are 269 numbered caves, with a mural area of about 10,000 square meters.

> 钟鼓楼

　　又名"林基路办公旧址"，位于乌什县热斯太西街10号。始建于清乾隆三十一年（1766年），历时一年完工。钟鼓楼呈四方形，因修建时的决策人物是伊犁将军明瑞，所以钟鼓楼的形制也和伊犁的惠远钟楼一样。钟鼓楼分两层，高14米，为砖木结构。

Bell and Drum Tower
Originally built in 1766, on the southeast side of the County's People's Government compound (Resi Taixi Street No.10), Uqturpan County, the brick and wood, two-storey towers are 14 meters high.

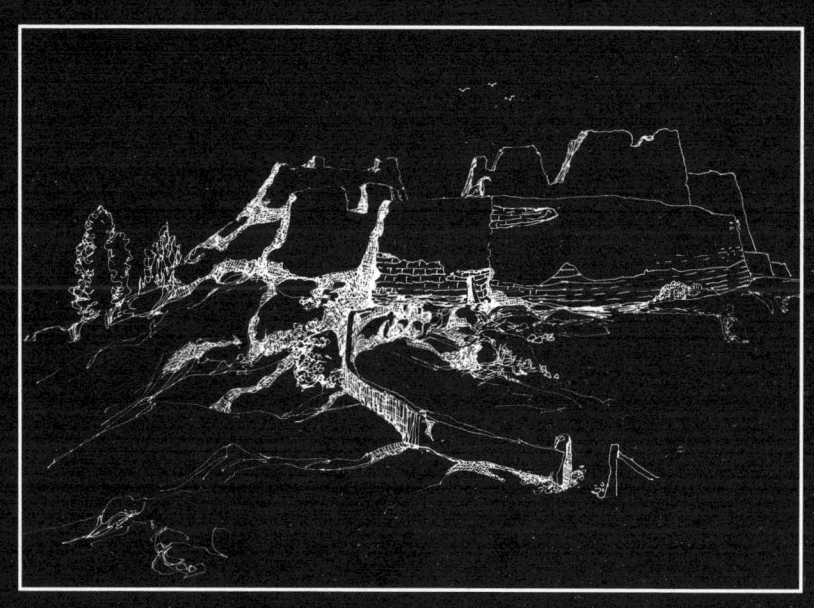

喀什地区
Kashgar Prefecture

徕宁城

　　位于喀什旧城西北约2000米处，始建于清乾隆二十七年（1762年），是清朝喀什噶尔参赞大臣的衙署。乾隆三十六年（1771年），皇帝赐该城名为"徕宁城"。该城设四门，城内有仓库、衙署、兵屋、教场、将台、关帝庙、万寿宫等建筑。图为徕宁城城门。

Laining Town
Originally built in 1762 2 kilometers northwest of old Kashgar, it was the government office of a Kashgar minister of the Qing Dynasty (1644-1911). Structures include four gates, a warehouse, a government office, and military barracks. The sketch shows Laining Town.

高台民居

位于喀什市老城区东北端,建在高40多米、长800多米黄土高崖上,是维吾尔族的聚居区,距今已有600多年的历史。房屋是用泥巴和杨木搭建而成的。木头去枝之后,没有刨削加工,直接用来架构和支撑屋顶、阁楼和阳台。

Gaotai Residents

"Gaotai", as an architecture style, indicates adding another story to a family home with each new generation. This house is located northeast of old Kashgar City, in the Uyghur concentrated areas on the loess cliffs that are more than 40 meters high, 800 meters long, with a history of over 600 years.

艾提尕尔清真寺·正门

位于喀什市艾提尕尔广场西侧，始建于明正统七年（1442年）。南北长140米，东西宽120米，占地总面积为1.68万平方米，分为正殿、外殿、教经堂、院落、拱拜孜、宣礼塔、大门等七部分。为新疆规模最大的清真寺，也是全国规模最大的清真寺之一。

Aitigaer Mosque · Main Entrance
Built in 1442 on the west side of Aitigaer square in Kashgar, it is 140 meters long north to south, and 120 meters wide east to west, covering an area of 16,800 square meters. It includes main hall, outer hall, teaching hall, courtyard, a Gongbaizi minaret, and main door.

艾提尕尔清真寺·塔楼

位于喀什市区艾提尕尔清真寺正门楼的两侧。由砖砌成，呈圆柱形，高12.5米，柱身环绕植物纹样和几何纹样，上修塔楼，塔楼顶部饰以弯月。

Atigaer Mosque · Tower Building

Located on both sides of the main entrance tower of Atigaer Mosque in Kashgar, it is a cylindrical brick structure 12.5 meters high.

香妃墓·正面

又名"阿帕克和卓麻扎",位于喀什市东郊5000米的浩罕村,始建于清康熙三十一(1692年),修建过程一直延续到20世纪初。"香妃墓"之称源于民间传说,香妃本名买木热·艾孜姆,自幼体有异香,被称为"伊帕尔罕"(香姑娘)。她被清朝皇帝选为妃子,赐号"香妃",因不服京城水土病故,运尸回乡,安葬于阿帕克霍加墓中。

Xiangfei Tomb · Front

Also named "Apak and Zhuomazar", it is in the Haohan Village five thousand meters from Kashgar. Originally founded in 1692, "Xiangfei Tomb" got its name from folklore. Xiangfei's real name was Maimure Aizimu, and since she was blessed with fragrance, she was given the name "Fragrant Concubine". When she died of an illness, her body was brought home and buried in the tomb of Apakhuojia.

> 香妃墓·背面

　　香妃墓建筑高40米，由门楼、小礼拜寺、大礼拜寺、教经堂和主墓室五部分组成。穹窿形的圆顶上，有一座塔楼。陵墓的厅堂里，筑有半人高的平台。香妃的坟丘设在平台的东北角。陵墓左边，建有大小两座精致的伊斯兰教礼拜寺。

Xiangfei Tomb · Rear Side

The 40-meter-high Xiangfei Tomb includes gate tower, pesantren, grand Friday mosque, teaching hall and main tomb built in the northeast corner of the platform. On the left side of the mausoleum, there are two fine Islamic Mosques. There is a graveyard behind the mausoleum.

:::阿巴哈加麻扎:::

　　位于喀什市的东北郊区，是传教士玉素甫·和加家族的麻扎。麻扎面积两万平方米，基墙四角有圆柱形塔柱和塔楼，还有门楼、"必修克"、大小礼拜寺、教经堂、水池等。图为麻扎内的大礼拜寺。

Abahajia Mazar
Located in Kashgar's northeastern suburb, it covers an area of 20,000 square meters. In the four corners of the base wall stand cylindrical columns and tower buildings, as well as a gate tower, "Bixiuke" (a tomb), mosques, a teaching hall, and a pool. The sketch shows the Grand Friday Mosque in Mazar.

三仙洞石窟遗址

维吾尔语为"玉素布尔杭",意为"三个佛教洞窟"。位于恰克玛克河南岸的断崖上,距离喀什市18千米左右,始建于东汉时期。洞口离地面20余米,离峭壁顶部八米,是中国西部保存较好的最古的佛教壁画洞窟。窟前建筑已不存,石窟为长方形,中间窟残存坐佛石胎,东窟残存少量壁画。

Sanxiandong Grottoes

Originally constructed during the Eastern Han Dynasty (25-220) in a cliff of the south bank of the Qiakemake River, it is about 18 kilometers from Kashgar. Of the grottoes remaining, three are rectangles in the middle of which are seated Buddhas; a few murals survive in the eastern caves.

莫尔佛塔寺院遗址

位于喀什市东北30千米处，始建于唐代。左侧是佛塔遗址，共分三层，塔基为方形，卵圆形土塔中空，残高12.8米；右侧是寺院遗址，长约25米，宽约21米，高约10米。10世纪初伊斯兰教正式传入喀什后，莫尔佛塔寺院在战火中消失。

Moer Pagoda Temple Ruins

Originally built during the Tang Dynasty (618-907) 30 kilometers northeast of Kashgar, the site includes a three-story On the left is the stupa with square base and an oval, hollow tower 12.8 meters high. On its right is the monastery, about 25 meters long, 21 meters wide, and 10 meters high.

| 阿勒通鲁克麻扎·全景 |

又名"莎车王陵",位于莎车县城的老城与旧城之间,始建于明嘉靖十二年(1533年),面积5000多平方米。该麻扎是叶尔羌汗国王族的陵墓,汗王苏力唐·赛义德、阿布都拉失德的陵园,音乐家阿曼尼莎罕也埋葬于此。

Aletongluke Mazar · Panorama
Also called "Shache Mausoleum", it was built in 1533 between the ancient and the old cities of Shache County. It had an area of more than 5000 square meters. The Mazar are the mausoleums of the Yarkand Khanate royal family and Khans Su Li Tang · Saeed and Abu Dhabi.

阿勒通鲁克麻扎·必修克

　　"必修克"即坟墓。阿勒通鲁克麻扎主要由清真寺、"必修克"、阿曼尼莎汗纪念堂、池塘四部分组成。墓区位于整个建筑群的中央位置，历代汗王的陵墓就位于周围有木质围栏的中央台子上。所有陵墓全部用青砖砌成，其上雕刻的各种图案至今仍清晰如新。

Aletongluke Mazar "Bixiuke"

"Bixiuke" refers to a tomb. This tomb area is located amidst all buildings; the ancient Khan's grey brick mausoleums sit in the central platform surrounded by wooden fences. The sketch shows the Aletongluke Mazar "Bixiuke".

加曼清真寺

位于莎车县莎车镇，始建于明永乐七年（1409年），叶尔羌汗国速檀·马合木汗在位时修建，阿古柏时期曾进行过整修。"加曼"的意思是"集体礼拜之处"。该建筑群前部为教经堂，后部为清真寺。门楼两侧各有半镶嵌在门楼中的圆形塔楼一个，门边墙上为凹面长方形和琼形。门楼内为穹顶，并绘有图案。

Garman Mosque

Located in Shache Town, Shache County, it was built in 1409. "Garman" means "a place of collective worship". The front of the complex is a teaching hall; behind is a mosque. A round tower stands on each side of the gate tower.

棋盘石窟

又名"棋盘千佛洞""姑娘洞",位于叶城县棋盘乡的山谷中,开凿时间至迟在10世纪以前,距今至少已有1000多年的历史。现残存十个石窟,初凿于西辽时期。洞窟为方形,顶部为拱状或覆斗状,最大的洞窟长4.4米、宽3.9米,最小的面积仅有两平方米。

Chessboard Grottoes

Located in a valley of Chessboard Township in Yecheng County, it is also known as "Chessboard Thousand-Buddha Cave" and "Girl Cave". This site dates back to almost 10th century. Now there are 10 caves excavated during the Western Liao period(1124-1218). The largest is 4.4 meters long and 3.9 meters wide; the smallest is only two square meters.

加曼清真寺

　　位于叶城县叶城镇，始建于明嘉靖十五年（1536年），上世纪曾先后维修过三次。该清真寺有礼拜大殿、宣礼楼、教经堂以及供礼拜者做"大小净"的场所，可供一万人在此做礼拜，是叶城县最大的一座清真寺。

Garman Mosque

Built in 1536 in Yecheng Town, Yecheng County, it is the largest in Yecheng County. It includes a great worship hall, a teaching hall, a manara, and washrooms for worshippers.

脱库孜萨来佛寺遗址

又称"吐木秀克",位于巴楚县托库孜萨来村,距离巴楚县城约75千米,始建于6世纪,出土的遗物有泥塑佛像、佛头范、汉文文书、龟兹文文书以及丝棉织品等。

Tuokuzisalai Buddhist Temple Site
Originally built in the 6th century in ancient Tuokuzisalai Town, about 75 kilometers from Bachu county, it is also called "Tumuxiuke". Unearthed relics here include clay Buddhist statues and various instruments and so on.

石头城

　　位于塔什库尔干县城以北400米处，海拔3100米，始建于汉代，唐至清代均有修缮和扩建。石头城建在山上，呈不规则四边形，北墙为土坯结构，东、西、南墙由石头砌筑而成。由城墙、城门、寺院、居住遗址和清代城堡等组成，面积10万多平方米，周长约1285米。

Stone Town

Originally built during the Han Dynasty (202 B.C.-220 A.D.) 400 meters north of Tashkurghan county at an elevation of 3,100 meters, the site consists of walls, gates, monasteries, residences, the Qing Dynasty (1644-1911) castles and covers an area of 100,700 square meters with a circumference of about 1,285 meters.

吉日尕尔汉唐驿站遗址

　　位于距离塔什库尔干县城约40千米处，始建于汉代，是汉唐之间的历史文化遗存。"吉日尕尔"在塔吉克语中即是"小站""驿站""旅店"的意思。

Jirigaer Han-Tang Inn Site

Originally built during the Han Dynasty (202 B.C.-220 A.D.) about 40 kilometers from Tashkurgan, it includes historical/cultural relics between the Han and Tang Dynasties (202B.C.-220, 618-907).

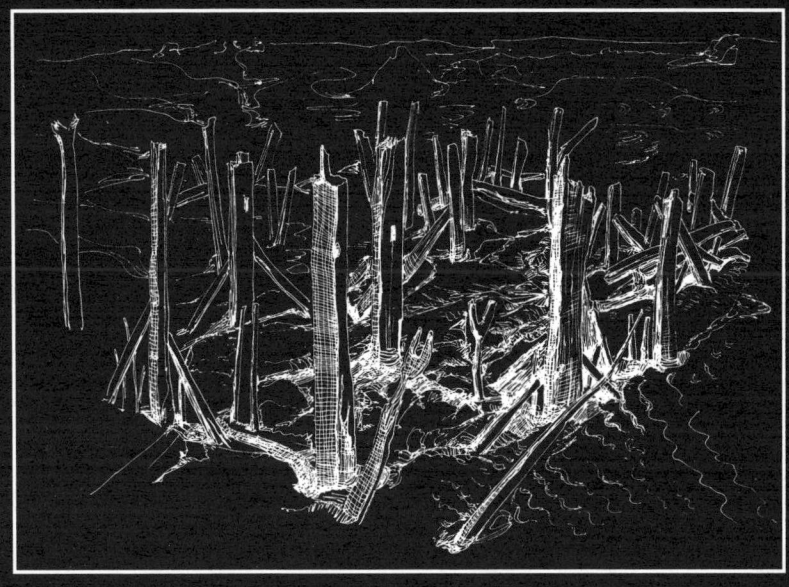

和田地区
Hotan Prefecture

热瓦克佛塔

　　位于洛浦县吉亚乡的库拉·坎斯曼沙漠中，距离洛浦县城60千米左右，维吾尔语意为"楼阁"或"亭台"。始建于魏晋时期，废弃于五代时期。佛塔用土块垒砌而成，基座为正方形，塔身为圆柱体，共有三层，目前残高近九米。

Rewake Pagoda

Originally built during the Wei and Jin Dynasties (220-265, 265-420), in Kula·Kansman desert, Jiya Town, Luofu County, about 60 kilometers from Luopu County, it was abandoned during the Five Dynasties period (907-960). The earthen pagoda has a square base and a 3-story cylindrical tower nearly 9 meters high.

阿克斯皮尔古城残墙

位于洛浦县城以北17千米处的沙漠中，兴建于汉代，废弃于宋代。"阿克斯皮尔"为维吾尔语，意为"白城堡"或"白城墙"。该城是一座具有军事防御功能的"坎城"，现仅存一段100米左右由土坯夯筑的弧形城墙。

The Ancient Town Wall of Akespier

Built during the Han Dynasty (202 B.C.-220 A.D.) in the desert 17 kilometers north of Luopu County, it was abandoned in the Song Dynasty (960-1276). Now only a 100-meter curved section of the adobe wall remains.

乌宗塔提遗址

又名"古媲摩遗址"，位于策勒县达玛沟乡北部沙漠中，在乡政府驻地北19千米处。始建于五代时期，遗址面积约100平方千米。遗址由南向北可以分为七个部分，其中房屋为土木结构，木框架式泥顶，墙壁抹泥，有些房址墙柱和门框尚存。文化层堆积厚度有些地方可达五米，内含灰土、陶片等。图为佛塔遗址。

Wuzongtati Site

Built during the Five Dynasties Period (907-960), in the desert north of Damago Township, Cele County, 19 kilometers from the north of township government, it has an area of about 100 square kilometers divided into seven parts south to north . The sketch shows the pagoda ruins.

流水墓地

位于于田县阿羌乡昆仑山深处流水村附近的阿克布拉克台地上，因村得名。距今约3000年，是首次在昆仑山北麓发现的青铜时代墓葬。墓葬多数为石围墓或石堆墓，墓葬形制多为竖穴土坑，出土的陶器多有刻划纹。

Liushui Cemetery

This Bronze Age cemetery located on Akebulake Plateau near Liushui Village Aqiang Town Yutian County in the depths of the Kunlun Mountains has a 3,000-year history. It is the first Bronze Age cemetery and earliest cultural relic found at the northern foot of the Kunlun Mountains.

> 喀拉墩故城

　　位于于田县克里雅河下游的三角洲地带的大河沿乡，距离于田县城约190千米。始建于汉代，是汉晋时期的扜弥国遗址，宋朝时废弃。古城呈长方形，面积5625平方米。遗址以喀拉墩城堡为中心，城堡四周有多处建筑群，多为民居、寺庙，在建筑群的附近有农田、渠道遗迹。

Karadong Site

Also called "Ancient Karadong Town", it was built during the Han Dynasty (202 B.C.-220 A.D) in Daheyan Township in the lower reaches of Keriya River delta of Yutian County. It is a Yumi state site of the Han and Jin Dynasties but abandoned during the Song Dynasty (960-1279). The rectangular town covers 5,625 square meters.

圆沙古城

又名"尤木拉克库木古城",位于于田县克里雅河下游的老河床东岸,始建于2000年前。古城呈不规则四边形,目前可见南面和东面城门,周长约995米,东西最宽处达270米。出土遗物有石器、陶片、铜器、铁器、玻璃、毛织物等。图为圆沙古城南门遗迹。

Ancient Yuansha Town

Also called " Ancient Town of Umulakekumu", it is located on the east bank of the lower reaches of Keriya River in Yutian County. Originally built in 2,000 years ago, the south and east gates of the ancient trapezoidal town remain visible. The town's circumference was about 995 meters - 270 meters at the widest part. The sketch shows the north gate of ancient Yuansha.

艾提卡尔大清真寺

位于于田县城内，始建于宋嘉熙元年（1237年），至今已进行过七次大规模的维修和扩建，总面积达1.34平方米，是于田县的标志性建筑。最多可容纳信众一万人以上。"艾提"为阿拉伯语"尔德"（节日）的变音；"卡"的波斯语意为"广场""位置"，两者合在一起,便成了"艾提卡"，即"节日场所"之意。

Aitikar Grand Mosque

Originally built in 1237 in Yutian County with a total area of 13,449 square meters, it is a local county landmark. "Aitikar" meaning "Festive Place" accommodate more than 10,000 people.

大清真寺

位于于田县城内,始建于清光绪十年(1884年)。其所采用的全封闭的空间组合形式成为现代清真寺的主要特征,在新疆伊斯兰建筑史上具有重要的意义。现该清真寺已成为当地重要的宗教活动场所。

Grand Mosque

Built in 1884 in Yutian County, its totally enclosed space combination is a major feature of modern mosques and of great significance in Xinjiang Islamic architectural history.

牛头山佛寺遗址

位于和田县城东南21千米处的喀拉喀什河东岸库玛尔山的崖壁上，古时因此山有两只状如牛角的突起，故被称作"牛头山"或"牛角山"。牛头山是于阗著名的佛教圣地，《大唐西域记》称其为"瞿室倰伽山寺"，是古代佛教徒心目中的灵鹫山，屡见于汉文史籍、汉译佛经、敦煌遗书乃至敦煌壁画中。

Niutou Mountain Buddhist Temple Site
Seated on Kumar Hill cliffs on the east bank of Karakash River, it is 21 kilometers southeast of Hetian County. In ancient times there were two geological formations like cattle horns; so, it is called "Cattle Head Mountain" or "Cattle Horn Mountain".

尼雅遗址·古城

　　位于民丰县城以北尼雅遗址的南部,因英国人斯坦因在尼雅河畔发现,被称为尼雅遗址。据考证该遗址为西域三十六国之一的精绝国老城,现周围被高大的红柳包所占据。据考,古城呈椭圆形,城墙由白色淤泥垛积而成,城门位于南城墙的中部,东西长185米,南北宽150米,周长约530米。

Niya Site · Jingjue Ancient Town

Built during the Wei/Jin Dynasties (220-265 and 265-420), south of the Niya site north of Minfeng County, it is also called Jingjue ancient capital. Amidst the oval shaped ruins, the gate is in the center of the south wall which is 185 meters long east to west, 150 meters wide north to south, and about 530 meters in circumference. The sketch is of Jingjue.

尼雅遗址·墓葬

位于尼雅遗址中，共发掘了八座属社会上层统治集团的墓葬，随葬品丰富、级别高，保存完好。按其种类可分为陶器、木器、铁器、漆器、弓矢、纺织品及料珠等，其中纺织品为其大宗，特别是出土了一批组织复杂、色彩绚烂、花纹繁缛的线织品和精美毛织品。图为墓葬。

Niya Site · Tombs
Amidst the Niya ruins, eight tombs of the ruling classes were found. Elegant well-preserved funerary objects found include pottery, woodwork, iron and lacquerware, bows and arrows, textiles, and beads and so on. The sketch shows the tomb.

尼雅遗址·佛殿

位于民丰县城以北尼雅遗址之中,佛殿平面为"回"字形,边长五米左右,殿堂中央为佛像,基座边长两米,行道宽1.1～1.4米。该佛殿出土物有铜饰件、木柱头、佛像和菩萨像壁画等。

Niya Site · Buddhist Hall
Located at the Niya site, north of Minfeng County, the hall is about 5 meters long. In the central hall sits a Buddha statue on a 2-meter base with a walking path 1.1-1.4 meters wide. The sketch shows the Buddhist Hall.

> 尼雅遗址·官署

　　位于民丰县城以北150千米的尼雅河畔，塔克拉玛干大沙漠的腹心地区。始建于西汉时期，距今大约2000年。古遗址以佛塔为中心，遗址内发现有房屋、场院、墓地、佛塔、佛寺、田地、果园、畜圈、河渠、陶窑、冶炼遗址等遗迹。图为尼雅遗址的官署。

Niya Site · Government Office
Built during the Western Han Dynasty (202 B.C.-25 A.D.) at the Niya River's end 150 kilometers north of the Minfeng county seat in the heart of the Taklamakan desert, it is an ancient Jingjue state site with 2,000-year history. The sketch shows Niya government office ruins.

安得悦古城

又名"开希米库勒",位于民丰县东部安迪尔河老河床的东岸,始建于唐代,城址呈圆形,直径约130米,城门在南,城墙用泥垛筑,墙基厚达九米多,残高有六米多。图为古城之佛塔遗址,佛塔基座为正方形,塔身为圆柱形,残高五米多。

Ancient Andeyue Town

Built during the Tang Dynasty (618-907) on the east bank of the Andier River in east Minfeng County, the town base has a 130-meter diameter. The gates in the south and the 9-meter-wide mud walls are over 6 meters high. The cylindrical Pagoda here on a square base is more than five meters high. The sketch shows pagoda ruins.

土墩子烽火台

　　位于阜康市天池乡六运村，距离阜康市4000米，距离六运古城16千米，始建于唐代，为唐代的耶勒守捉城。烽火台呈梯形，夯筑，残高四米。周围散布有红、灰陶片，烽火台西侧有古老的建筑遗迹。

Tudunzi Beacon Tower

Built during the Tang Dynasty (618-907) in Liuyun Village, Tianchi Town four kilometers from Fukang City, and sixteen kilometers from ancient Liuyun, it has a trapezoidal rammed earth beacon tower. Each rammed earth layer of the tower's remaining 4 meters is 6.8 centimeters.

土墩子清真寺

　　位于阜康市第六师土墩子农场场部团结路20号，距离阜康市区约20千米，始建于1894年。整个大寺占地面积435平方米，建筑面积235平方米，坐西向东，平面布局呈"凸"字形，建筑形式为勾连搭式，重梁起架，飞檐斗拱，是新疆少见的有斗拱的砖木结构清真寺。

Tudunzi Mosque

Built in 1894 at No. 20 Tuanjie Road, Tudunzi Farm, about 20 kilometers from Fukang City, the mosque grounds covers an area of 435 square meters with a construction area of 235 square meters. It is the only Xinjiang mosque with brick and wood brackets.

北庭西大寺

又名"北庭佛寺""回鹘佛寺",位于吉木萨尔县城,始建于唐代,为高昌回鹘王国皇家寺院遗址。佛寺残迹平面呈长方形,南北长约70.5米,东西宽约43.8米。整个建筑分南北两个部分,南面为庭院、配殿、僧房、库房等建筑群;北面为正殿,其四周筑洞窟,窟内残留有高昌回鹘时期的壁画若干。

North Court West Temple

Also called "North Court Buddhist Temple" and "Uighur Temple", it was built during the Tang Dynasty (618-907) one kilometer west of the North Court Supervision Office. The royal Gaochang Uighur monastery site is rectangular, 70.5 meters north-south, 43.8 meters east-west.

巴音郭楞蒙古自治州
Bayingol Mongolian Autonomous Prefecture

铁门关遗址

位于孔雀河上游霍拉山与库鲁克山夹峙的沟谷，距离库尔勒市8000米左右。始建于晋代，初因其地势险固被称作"铁门关"。该遗址南北长100米、宽30米，残存有十余间以卵石垒砌的房屋。

Iron Gate Site
Built during the Jin Dynasty (265-420) atop of the hill between Mt. Uhuola and Kuru Hill, in the upper reaches of Peacock River 8 kilometers from Korla, it was originally about 100 meters long north to south, 30 meters wide east to west. There are more than ten cobblestone houses here.

拉依苏汉代烽燧遗址

  位于轮台县城以西约20千米的荒漠中，始建于汉代。该遗址由夯筑而成，残高四米左右，边长约六米，其主要功能是获悉军事情报和防御外敌入侵。烽火台南侧附近残存有房屋遗迹，曾出土规整较多剪轮五铢铜钱，烽火台四周残存有屯田遗址。

Han Dynasty Layisu Beacon Tower Site

Built to collect military intelligence and defend against invasion of enemies during the Han Dynasty (202 B.C.-220 A.D.), it is in the desert 20 kilometers west of Luntai County. The ruins of rammed earth are about 4 meters high.

| 拉依苏唐代烽燧遗址 |

位于拉依苏河畔，距离轮台县城约24千米，始建于唐代。该烽燧由土坯垒砌而成，台基平面呈正方形，边长13米，残高14米，附近有戍堡。该遗址出土有铁刀、箭镞、铁制农具、货币、铜镜等器物。

Tang Dynasty Layisu Beacon Tower Site

Built during the Tang Dynasty (618-907) on the banks of Layisu River about 24 kilometers from the Luntai County seat, the site's base plane is square, 13 meters wide, 14 meters high. Objects unearthed here include iron knives, arrowheads, iron tools, coins, and bronze mirrors.

营盘古城遗址

位于尉犁县城约150千米的甘草厂附近的崖壁上，距离，始建于东汉时期。该城在古代是从敦煌经楼兰深入西域腹地的孔道，被誉为"第二楼兰"。古城呈圆形，直径约60米，大部分为夯土建筑，主要由城址、佛寺、烽燧、墓地等组成。

Ancient Yingpan Town Site

Built during the Eastern Han Dynasty (25-220), on cliffs near headquarters of the 35th Regiment, 2nd Division, Production and Construction Corps in Xinjiang, about 150 kilometers from Yuli county seat, the round town site is 60 meters in diameter. The rammed-earth structures of the site include Buddhist temples and cemeteries.

小河墓地·女性墓

位于若羌县孔雀河的支流——小河的东侧，总面积约2500平方米，始建于公元前2000年。墓葬由多层次堆积而成，最多的叠压了五层，多数棺前树立着象征男根或女阴的立木以及涂着红颜色的高大木桩。图为女性墓。

Xiaohe Cemetery · Female Tomb
Built in 2000 BC on the east bank of a river in Ruoqiang County, it has an area of 2,500 square meters The site has many layers; in front of most of the graves are trees symbolizing male and female and tall stakes painted red. The sketch shows women's tomb.

楼兰古城·三间房遗址

　　位于若羌县的罗布泊西岸，面积有11万多平方米，始建于2000年前。楼兰古城为方形土城，该遗址出土了大量汉文、佉卢文文书，另有木雕佛像、货币、陶器、铜镜、漆器、锦等遗物。图为楼兰古城的"三间房"遗址。

Loulan Ancient Town · Three Rooms site

Built 2,000 years ago on Lake Lop Nor's west shore in Ruoqiang County, covering an area of 110,000 square meters, it was constructed of square rammed earth. Many documents, carved Buddha statues, coins and other relics have been unearthed here. The sketch shows the "Three Rooms" site.

楼兰古城·佛塔遗址

　　位于楼兰古城的东北区，残高10米左右，塔基为方形，塔身为八角形，塔顶为覆钵式。该遗址出土了大量的木雕坐佛像、木刹柱等佛教遗物。图为佛塔遗址。

Ancient Loulan Town · Pagoda Site
Located northeast of Loulan, it is about 10 meters high. Many carved Buddha statues, wooden columns and Buddhist relics were unearthed here. The sketch shows the pagoda site.

孔雀河古墓沟

又名"太阳墓",位于孔雀河下游北岸第二台地上,东距干涸的罗布泊约70千米,距今3800年左右。墓葬平面结构呈环形,共列七圈木桩,葬者多为男性,遗物有玉珠手链、木雕人像、草编器具、骨器、动物角、铜器等。

Peacock River Ancient Grave Ditch

Also called "Sun Tomb", it is located on the second plateau of the north bank of the lower reaches of Peacock River about 70 kilometers west of Lop Nor lake. With a history of 3,800 years, the tomb's ring-shaped base is surrounded by seven circles of wooden stakes. Most men are buried here.

米兰佛寺

位于若羌县米兰河流域，共有近20座寺院和佛塔，始建于东汉中晚期，是我国现存最早的佛教寺院。寺院采取前塔后殿的建筑布局，佛殿以"窣堵坡"为中心。

Milan Buddhist Temple
Built during the middle to late Eastern Han Dynasty (25–220) in the Milan water basin of Ruoqiang County, the temples and pagodas number twenty. The earliest Buddhist temple in China is among them.

奎克衙门（和静县民族博物馆）

又名"满楚克扎布汗王爷府"或"满汉王府"，位于和静县城中心。始建于1927年，曾是蒙古南路土尔扈特部四旗二十七代汗王满楚克扎布的最高权力机构。该建筑现仅存正殿和东西两宫，面积1000平方米左右，现为和静县民族博物馆。

Quike Government Office

Also called "Manchukezhabu Khan Royal Highness House" or "Manhan Royal Highness House", it was built in 1927 in Henjing county. The main hall and east and west palaces, with an area of about 1,000 square meters, remain.

察吾乎古墓群石围石室墓

位于和静县哈尔莫墩乡觉伦吐尔根村察吾乎沟附近的台地上，距今约3200年，是新疆青铜时代文化的典型代表。该墓室为椭圆形竖穴，由卵石砌筑而成，双人合葬，仰身屈肢，有陶器等陪葬品。

Chawuhu Ancient Stone Tombs

Located on a plateau near Chawuhu Trench, in Jueluntuergen Village, Haermodun Township, Hejing County, the 3,200-year-old tombs are oval, vertical caves filled with pebbles so as to double the capacity of bodies buried erect amid pottery and other funerary objects.

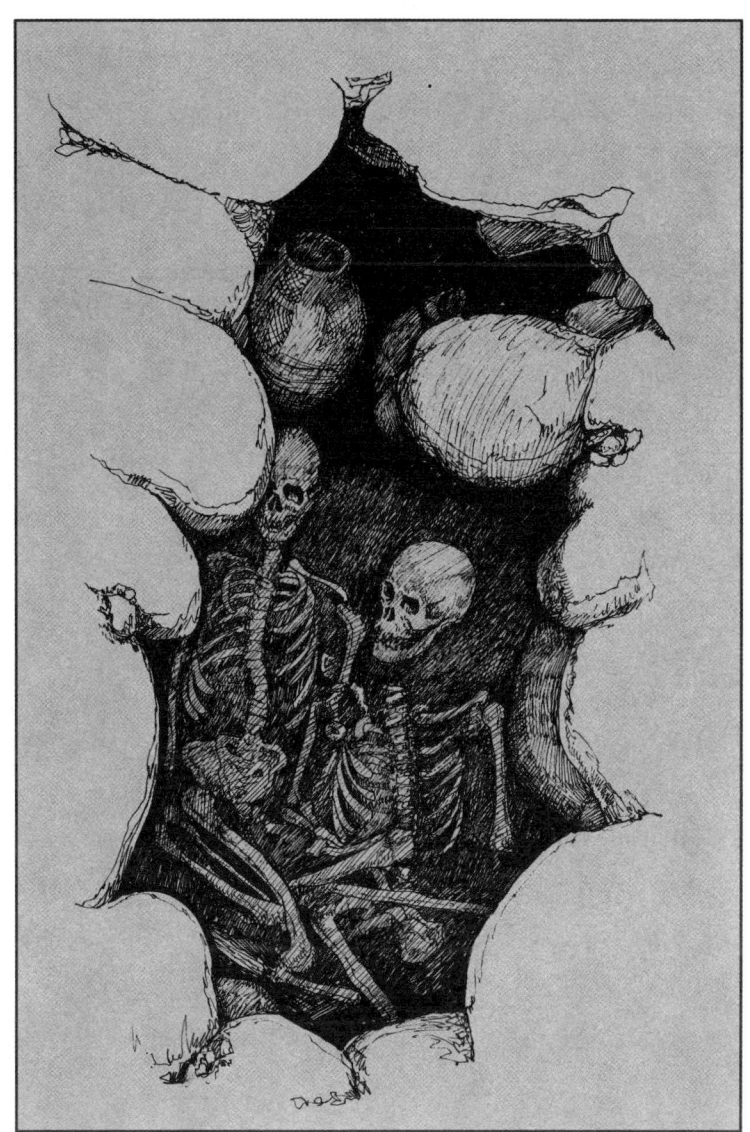

奥巴尔墓地石人

又名"阿尔夏特石人"。位于和静县巴音布鲁克风景区阿尔夏特村,为8~9世纪遗物。石人为男性,露出地面部分高约80厘米,脸型为长方形,五官明显,两臂弯曲。

Obaer Cemetery Stone Man

Located on Obaer Cemetery, Aerxiate Village, Bayinbuluke scenic area, Hejing county, it has relics of the 8th and 9th centuries. The exposed part of the Stone Man is about 80 centimeters above ground.

| 黄 庙 |

　　位于和静县巴仑台镇以南约18千米处，建于清光绪十四年（1888年）。该庙是蒙古南路土尔扈特部的总庙，全盛时期面积达1.4万平方米，现面积有2500平方米，主体建筑由大殿和双塔构成。

Huang Temple
Built during the reign of Emperor Guangxu (1875-1909), about 18 kilometers south of Baluntai, Hejing county with an area of 2500 square meters, its main buildings are the great hall and twin towers.

伊犁哈萨克自治州
Ili Kazak Autonomous Prefecture

陕西回族大寺

原名"宁固寺",又名"凤凰寺""金顶寺""陕甘大寺"。位于伊宁市汉人街,始建于清乾隆二十五年(1760年)。该寺仿照陕西省西安市化觉巷清真寺修建,采用中国传统建筑工艺,兼有阿拉伯伊斯兰风格。寺院以礼拜殿为主体建筑,分外殿、中殿、里殿。殿前后、两侧分别有卷棚、走廊。

Shaanxi Hui Grand Temple
Built in 1760 on Hanren Street, Yining City, it has traditional Chinese, Arabic and Islamic architectural styles.

六星街

位于伊宁市内,始建于1934年,是一处集中展示俄罗斯族传统文化的历史街区。20世纪三四十年代,这里的俄罗斯侨民占居民总数的60%,后大部分侨民都已离开。目前这里居住着维吾尔族、俄罗斯族、塔塔尔族等少数民族。这里的俄罗斯特色建筑都得到了很好的保存。图为六星街的俄罗斯学校。

Six Star Street
Built in 1934 in Yining City, the street is a historic district displaying Russian traditional culture; the typical Russian architecture is well preserved. The sketch shows a Russian school on this street.

伊犁将军府

位于霍城县惠远乡惠远古城中心，始建于清光绪八年（1882年）。将军府坐北朝南，整个建筑为四合院式，主要建筑有军府大门、将军府正殿、将军亭、东西营房、客房、书房等。图为伊犁将军府钟鼓楼。

General Ili's Mansion
Built in 1882 in ancient Huiyuan's center Huiyuan Township, in Huocheng County, the general's south-facing mansion includes gate, government hall, the general booth, east and west barracks, and guest and study rooms. The sketch shows its Bell and Drum Tower.

吐虎鲁克麻扎

位于霍城县新疆生产建设兵团第四师75团，建于元至正二十五年（1365年），是成吉思汗的七世孙、东察合台汗王吐虎鲁克·铁木耳的陵墓。墓祠平面呈长方形，正面宽10.8米、进深15.8米。正中为一穹窿顶，祠内有暗梯。墓祠正面入口呈尖拱式，除门楣和门边用阿拉伯文装饰外，其余用紫、白、蓝色琉璃镶砌，琉璃面砖组成各种图案和花纹。

Tuhuluke Mazar

Built in 1365, Tuhulukemazar is located in 75th Regiment, 4th Division, Xinjiang Production and Construction Corps area of Huocheng county. It is the mausoleum of Thhuluke Temur, King of Eastern Chahatai, the 7th-generation descendant of Genghis Khan. The domed tomb is rectangular, 10.8 meters wide, 15.8 meters deep and has a hidden ladder.

惠远古城

　　位于伊犁河北岸的广阔平原上，距离霍城县城15千米左右，始建于1882年，是清朝统一新疆后伊犁将军的驻地，也是"伊犁九城"中面积最大的一座城池。沙俄入侵伊犁后，惠远城被毁，现仅存东墙、西墙、将军府和钟鼓楼。

Ancient Huiyuan Town

Built in 1882, Huiyuan is located on the vast plains on the north bank of the Ili River about 15 kilometers from Huocheng. It is the Yili General's garrison after unifying Xinjiang during the Qing Dynasty (1644-1911). Now only the east and west walls, the General's House and the Bell and Drum Towers remain.

昭苏县草原石人

位于昭苏县，为唐代遗物。石人共九座，图中的石人雕刻的是突厥武士形象。石人为花岗岩材质，五官及表情清晰可见，左手握刀，右手持酒杯。

Grassland Stone Men in Zhaosu County

These are Tang Dynasty (618-907) relics. Among the nine stone men, the one in the sketch is a Turkic warrior. Made of granite, the figure holds a knife in its left hand, a wine glass in its right.